welcome one another

A HANDBOOK FOR
HOSPITALITY MINISTERS

Paul E. Hoffman

Augsburg Fortress

WELCOME ONE ANOTHER
A Handbook for Hospitality Ministers

Also available:

Leading Worship Matters: A Sourcebook for Preparing Worship Leaders (ISBN 978-1-4514-7806-8)
Praying for the Whole World: A Handbook for Intercessors (ISBN 978-1-5064-1596-3)
Serving the Assembly's Worship: A Handbook for Assisting Ministers (ISBN 978-1-4514-7808-2)
Getting the Word Out: A Handbook for Readers (ISBN 978-1-4514-7807-5)
Altar Guild and Sacristy Handbook, 4th rev. ed. (ISBN 978-1-4514-7809-9)
Worship Matters: An Introduction to Worship (Participant book ISBN 978-1-4514-3605-1;
    Leader guide ISBN 978-1-4514-3604-4)

Cover design: Laurie Ingram
Cover photo: Copyright © Pearl/Lightstock
Interior design: Ivy Palmer Skrade
Editor: Suzanne Burke

Manufactured in the U.S.A.

ISBN 978-1-5064-1597-0

20   19   18   17   16   1   2   3   4   5

Contents

So [Paul and Barnabas and some of the others] were sent on their way by the church, and as they passed through both Phoenicia and Samaria, they reported the conversion of the Gentiles, and brought great joy to all the believers. When they came to Jerusalem, they were welcomed by the church and the apostles and the elders, and they reported all that God had done with them.

Acts 15:3-4

It starts in the parking lot
That most important first welcome

What are the initial impressions of any worshiper who pulls into your parking lot at a time of worship? Or, for that matter, in a more urban setting, one who hops off the bus or walks up to the front door?

Are the grounds neatly kept, a mirror of the beauty of creation? Is ample parking available? Is it clear where one should park? Is the lot littered with specialized signs: Pastor's Parking; Musician's Parking; Visitor's Parking? Once one has arrived, is it clear where to enter the building, and are the doors of that entrance clearly marked and unlocked? Do they offer the newcomer and the seasoned worshiper alike a wide welcome to the worshiping assembly?[1]

---

1 Richard Reising, *What If Starbucks Marketed Like the Church: A Parable* (https://www.youtube.com/watch?v=D7_dZTrjw9I), is an instructive, entertaining look at some of these very questions and many more from the chapters yet to come.

It's often hard for us to see the forest for the trees—the familiarity of our church home makes it difficult for us to evaluate and take meaningful action on the questions offered above. The weeds in the median are so familiar to us, it's difficult to see them as a first-time worshiper might: a sign of lack of care and concern for the Creator's place of worship.

To honestly evaluate what fresh eyes see in both parking lot exterior upkeep and even the gathering space itself, consider inviting a team from a neighboring congregation to visit a hospitality team meeting and gently comment on what they experience at your place of worship as first-time visitors. What do they see that you can no longer see? How do they experience this initial stage of visiting your congregation?

In a gracious effort to build up all of the body of Christ, offer this invitation with the corresponding proposition of visiting *their* congregation to do the same. Whether this is the United Methodist congregation down the street or another ELCA congregation in the next county, to do this work together for the good of the gospel is a holy thing.

As a first step in evaluating the welcome of your outdoor surroundings and parking areas, come up with a checklist as you survey your grounds with the eyes of a newcomer. Be creative and thorough in your analysis. Such an evaluation can be both uplifting and instructive. Enter into it with the mind of Christ, and then invite some neighbors to have a look with your checklist in hand.

When Paul and Barnabas and the others traveled through Phoenicia and Samaria and on into Jerusalem for one of the church's most important early conversations, the book of Acts makes it clear that there was joyous welcome all along their route. Especially when they reached their final destination in Jerusalem, *they were welcomed by the church and the apostles and the elders.* It doesn't say that everyone was there in the parking lot to greet them, but wouldn't that be a wonderful sight if every Sunday at our places of worship that were able to happen? Even if we can't all be there as each car or SUV pulls in, as each person gets off the bus or subway, as families of all sorts of configurations come up the sidewalk, what if the surroundings they encountered were as welcoming as the people themselves might be?

"What is all the fuss?" you might ask. "People are perfectly capable of getting from the parking lot to the front door. They don't even notice what things look like." That may be true. But it also may *not* be true.

Consider what it might be like to you to be a newcomer at an unfamiliar and holy place. If you were to arrive at a mosque or a synagogue, would you feel confident about your next move? By which door should you enter? Are there separate doors for men and women? Once inside, is any special dress required? Head covering? Shoes on or off? Most Christians would not know the answer to these questions and, consequently, most would feel reluctant to attend a memorial service, wedding, or special event—even if specifically invited.

We once believed that as a majority culture in North America everyone knew all there was to know about a church and its surroundings. That was probably never fully true. But it certainly is no longer true in a post-Christian North American culture. Most people in our towns and cities, in the neighborhoods and surrounding countryside of our church properties are completely mystified about who we are, what we do, and who is welcome—or not. Carefully attending to that first brush with all things Christian beginning in the parking lot is a critical consideration. To do so is to extend to all who may come to inquire about Jesus the very first bit of welcome to a life of faith.

"

Whoever welcomes you
welcomes me, and whoever
welcomes me welcomes
the one who sent me.

Matthew 10:40

Greeters in the gathering space
The hub of hospitality

Once inside the door, the first impressions from external surroundings are about to be replaced with the best gift of all—genuine human contact. If we believe the words of Jesus recorded in the Gospel of Matthew, then what is about to happen is not just a handshake and a pat on the back. It is the connection between Christ and Christ's people that is offered by ushers and greeters. Imagine it! You who have chosen to serve in these roles are ambassadors for Christ.

More than the door: making connections

I'm going to go way out on a limb here and suggest that there may be a more effective and genuine way of offering such a profound greeting than by being positioned directly in front of the entrance door and regimented by worn words of repeated welcome, "Good morning. Good morning. Good morning."

What if assigned greeters were more in the role of minglers? Jessicah Krey Duckworth, in *Wide Welcome*, draws on the work of Penelope Eckert and Etienne Wenger. She elaborates on their coined term *brokers* for parish leaders who spend much of their ministry making connections from person to person.[2] I'd like to expand that vision to imagine it as the work of every welcoming coworker of Christ. Certainly it can be the important work of a Sunday hospitality team.

With a well-trained eye toward making connections, the assigned greeters for the day might find themselves, instead of firmly positioned directly inside the main entrance doors, as persons who move about the gathering space and help people to make connections that welcome and invite:

> *"Welcome to our worship this morning. I don't think we've met before . . ."*

> *"I see you have two small children. Mary and John should be here any minute. They have kids just about*

2 Jessicah Krey Duckworth, *Wide Welcome: How the Unsettling Presence of Newcomers Can Save the Church* (Minneapolis: Fortress Press, 2013), 91ff.

this age. Maybe you know them from Freedom Elementary School."

"Hi, I'm Mirin Kishina. I've been worshiping here at Gift of Grace for a little over a year now. I'm glad you're here. It can be challenging to step into a brand new place."

"Wow. You moved here to work for John Deere just north of town? Let me introduce you to Evan Davis. He's worked there for years."

"This is your first time at a Lutheran service? Would you like someone to help you navigate? Imran just began worshiping with us last summer. I think he'd be a wonderful worship partner for you your first time through."

These sorts of greetings offer much broader opportunity to making human connection than the easily repeated, "Good morning." More, they appear to be deeper and more genuine, making the kind of human connection that characterizes a community in Christ. Many who walk through our doors these days are disturbed and sometimes even angered by the institutionalization of church. Some are deeply hurt. Those "trying out" congregational life again or for the first time will find these deeper greetings more authentic and therefore more welcoming.

With such encouragement for connecting folks one to another also comes a warning. Many people who come to explore the possibility of Christian worship, or even the deeper possibility of discipleship, prefer an anonymous entrance into the worship experience. Such folks will often come five to ten minutes after the announced starting time of worship and will often leave prior to the service's ending, sometimes even shortly after the sermon.

The sensitive hospitality team will be attuned to such visitors, finding that fine line between offering a genuine welcome and offering so much information and connection as to overwhelm. Be kind to yourselves. You will not always get it exactly right. Count on the power of the gospel to take up the slack.

Where possible, it is an added bonus to have the vested presider among those offering greeting and welcome to the liturgy of the baptized. Her or his role is not to replace that of the ushers and greeters, but to enhance and amplify it. More, the presence of the vested presider as the congregation gathers helps longtime worshiper and newcomer alike to make the connection between the conversation of the world and the proclamation of the word at the font, ambo, and table. Few gifts of ministry can be as compelling to newcomers as to be greeted by name by the presider as they arrive for worship and then welcomed again by name to the table in the sharing of the eucharist.

A trained group of greeters, such as those envisioned here, can begin to make the gathering space the true nexus of the kingdom of God—the place where the world and the word meet. "The narthex [gathering space] serves as a significant transition area that can promote or discourage hospitality.[3]

Assess your gathering space

As we considered in chapter 1 on the external environment, let's have a look at the gathering space of your congregational home. Whether a storefront, a house church, or a cathedral, the environment of the transition space between the outside world and the place of worship is a significant factor in setting the tone for worship.

Consider clutter. Many entrances and gathering spaces become catchalls for congregational clutter. Forgotten hats, coats, and umbrellas; bulletin boards filled with

3 Walter C. Huffman and S. Anita Stauffer, *Where We Worship* (Philadelphia: Board of Publication, Lutheran Church in America, 1987), 29.

out-of-date announcements; overflowing congregational mailboxes; even dead plants and flowers are not uncommon sights in the spaces appointed for welcome and transition in our congregational homes.

In place of these expected surroundings so common in most congregational gathering spaces, consider instead simple, gracious, and inexpensive decor that truly aids in making the transition from world to word. Such surroundings could include but not be limited to:

> *swaths of cloth in the liturgical color of the season*
> *candles*
> *a table with the eucharistic gifts to be presented at the offering*
> *seasonal artwork*
> *local floral gifts*
>> *bare twigs in Advent*
>> *evergreen at Christmas and Epiphany*
>> *gnarled branches during Lent*
>> *spring flowers throughout the Easter season*
>> *gifts of the garden in summer*
>> *fruits of the harvest in late summer and autumn's ordinary time*

One of the items of clutter in many gathering spaces is a collection of name tags. Though wildly popular, name tags work at cross-purposes with building relationships in congregational worship by actually inhibiting rather than encouraging conversation and deeper relationships. Further, they immediately classify those in attendance as *insiders* and *outsiders*. If you have one, you obviously belong here. If you do not, the message subliminally communicated is "you do not." Even if provisions are made to provide visitors or newcomers with a name tag, they will of necessity be different than those of the established congregation, thereby creating a stratification of participants. More, many visitors do not care to be identified by name, and they certainly are not looking forward to having a name tag handed to them with the expectation that it will be worn. More invasive yet is the practice of having a name tag placed or pinned on you as you enter the gathering.

Thoughtful attention

In the same way, thought and care should be taken to the propriety of having guests stand to introduce themselves in the liturgical setting. For those who have been in and around church and its practices for many years or perhaps even a lifetime, it is difficult to imagine how overwhelming such a request can be for a newcomer. More, many people really do wish to remain somewhat anonymous as they enter into congregational life. The pressure to self-identify and speak publicly can be very intimidating to those who are new to holy spaces. Returning again to the example of the mosque or synagogue from chapter 1, imagine what it might be like for you to be asked to stand, introduce yourself, and speak in that setting.

Similar principles apply to a parish guest book. Expecting that persons attending worship would automatically wish to publically disclose their full names and personal information (address, phone, email) is unreasonable. Yet securing that information for future contact is a reasonable and good practice. Methods of gathering that information are discussed in the appendix, where a sample "Count Me In" form is also offered for replication.

Perhaps the team from a neighboring congregation that has come by to help you assess your exterior can come inside and continue their "first impressions" evaluation of your gathering space surroundings. A further worthy experiment would be to invite three or four persons from your community to a regular meeting of your hospitality team to listen carefully as they speak about what it might be like for them to enter into congregational spaces for the first time. Such a meeting would need to be carefully constructed to be an opportunity for *listening*, not a forum for defending current practice. Your team working together can learn a great deal by forming a list of questions then sharing them with those invited a week prior to their appointed meeting time with you.

With a group of men and women of all ages, along with teens and children who are trained to carry out their ministry of welcome in this way—rather than as door greeters—the gathering space for worship becomes a hub of preservice activity, conversation, and invitation. Beyond the "assigned" greeters of the day who might take primary responsibility for attending to all who enter the sacred space, over time an entire congregation comes to heartily extend the sorts of welcome, guidance, and invitation described above. Who knows? Maybe sooner or later the ministry of greeters could fade away altogether, replaced by a congregation that is nimble and generous in its ability to delight in all who gather, connecting them to one another. And, ultimately, connecting them to God.

The gifts [Christ] gave were
that some would be apostles,
some prophets, some
evangelists, some pastors
and teachers, to equip the
saints for the work of
ministry, for building up the
body of Christ, until all of us
come to the unity of the faith
and of the knowledge of the
Son of God, to maturity, to
the full measure of the full
stature of Christ.

Ephesians 4:11-13

Orchestrating order
The ministry of ushers

What joy to be the people who have volunteered for or been appointed to equip the saints for the work of ministry. I'll be the first to admit that the Ephesians' list of workers in the kingdom of God does not include ushers, but their role is written between every line. These blessed men and women offer themselves week in and week out to equip the saints for the first work of ministry—the worship of the triune God. Their work is so much more than simply handing out bulletins and collecting the offering.

In addition to all of the greeting ministries in the previous chapter, the ushers are the last to interact with the worshiping community prior to its gathering in assembly. Offering a greeting that is warm and inviting, but that also bears in mind the gravity of what is about to happen in worship is the perfect mind-set for the ministry of the usher. A worship greeting on Easter Sunday will have a different character and content than that on Ash Wednesday. Those who greet and usher at weddings have a distinctively different vocation than those who do so for a funeral or memorial liturgy.

Getting ready

Prior to the arrival of the worshiping community, the ushers have essential tasks of hospitable welcome to attend to as they prepare for their congregational service. Together with the greeting team, they should have a pre-negotiated list of routine duties that are absolutely essential to a wide welcome: doors unlocked, garbage emptied, toilets flushed, temperature controlled, lights appropriately adjusted. The welcome team's ongoing familiarity with directions to the nursery, accessibility options, restrooms, drinking fountains, coat closets, and the like are essential. Sometimes these tasks seem so routine that they are forgotten or neglected. Don't let them be. Many visitors will tell you that the two most important rooms for forming a first impression about a congregation are not the sanctuary or the gathering space, but the nursery and the restrooms.

Not everyone who comes to worship on any given occasion will be there because they are filled with joy and gratitude. Bear in mind that some you greet will just have received one of life's bitterest blows: the end of a marriage, the death of a loved one, the loss of a job, a shocking diagnosis. Your work is to equip *each* of them for the work of ministry that lies ahead—liturgy, which is by its very definition *the work of the people.*

Equipping for liturgy in many places will mean distributing a printed order of worship. In other settings it will mean directing people's attention to screens or other means of following liturgical patterns. For newcomers and latecomers, having hymnals at the ready with worship orders already inserted in the beginning pages is a great aid to their worship. Such preparation provides a gentle entry for the latecomer and a less anxious engagement with the worshiping community.

Ushers will also want to have in mind easily accessible seating for the needs of those who are arriving. Where is the accessible seating? Where are seats available for a larger family or a visiting group? Can the usher sense whether leading folks to those seats would be a welcome gesture or would draw unwanted attention to those trying to arrive without fanfare?

Staying tuned in

Much of the usher's task depends on a great sense of familiarity with the space and customs of the assembly, and a cultivated sense of intuition about the needs of those who are entering into worship. While many who volunteer for this ministry are by nature highly extroverted, it is good to bear in mind that often God's people arrive for worship in the hope of being lost in their own thoughts, prayers, and desires for their encounter with the Holy One.

Sometimes the conviviality of visiting with other ushers or with familiar friends and neighbors distracts ushers from the sort of welcome and duty they are called on to provide for everyone who enters into worship. A newcomer or first-time visitor will feel like an outsider if greeted off-handedly by a huddle of old friends having a jovial conversation. What is needed is a warm welcome, a hymnal, and an order of worship.

As the liturgy progresses, it is likely that the greeters will be seated with the assembly, but the ushers continue to serve in the gathering space, welcoming later arriving worshipers, assisting those who leave the worship with directions toward their needed area, assisting in the event of a medical emergency, and providing a watchful but still welcoming eye should anyone wish to enter the building with harmful intent.

Emergencies

Certainly ushers do not need to be as trained as first responders, and yet there is a rare but real possibility that they could be called on to care for the safety of a congregation in the face of an egregious emergency. Since settings and possibilities around this unlikely eventuality vary so widely, I suggest a consultative conversation with someone in your direct community who has training in maintaining the safety of gathered groups—perhaps a school principal, a factory supervisor, or a nursing home administrator. Such a conversation could equip the ushering team to be better prepared to respond proactively in a crisis rather than having to regret their actions or inaction later.

Communion

At an appropriate time in the liturgy, the ushers will no doubt be called on to receive the congregation's offerings, present them to the table, and—depending on local ritual custom—present the eucharistic gifts as well. Such duties should be carried out in a way that is simple and dignified, with an attitude appropriate to the gravity of the giving and receiving of precious gifts. In some smaller congregational settings, each worshiper may bring her or his offering to the table. Members of the altar guild or others who have prepared the table may be the ones to offer the bread and wine.

Directing God's people to the table to receive the holy gifts of bread and cup are sometimes the responsibility of the ushering servants as well. While meant to offer all who gather an orderly way to approach the table, usher instructions can sometimes be overly complicated. I sometimes wonder what would happen if we simply let the community—particularly in smaller worshiping congregations—come to the table as each worshiper felt called to do so by the Spirit. Would there be anarchy or simply a beautifully self-choreographed ebb and flow of God's people who come to the table as they feel called and enjoy the freedom to stay at the table for prayer and meditation as long as they desire?

Gracious welcome to the table, if ushers *do* serve as directive guides (as in many larger congregations), should be practiced abundantly. There is a critical difference between a gesture of an extended arm gently indicating a direction and a rigid arm with a pointed finger. A nod and a smile can often accomplish more than voluminous verbal instructions, and do so with a fuller measure of grace and warmth.

Other duties

In some assemblies the ushers have the responsibility of counting those in attendance. A worship team might first ask if this traditional responsibility is actually necessary. Could the number of persons gathered for worship, if it's needed at all, be ascertained some other way? In any event, counting should never be made obvious nor become a distraction from the liturgical action. It is simply inappropriate, for example, to have ushers with clipboards and pencils moving in the side aisles and obviously counting heads during the reading of the scriptures or the praying of congregational prayers.

As with greeters, those ushers who are "off duty" because it is not their assigned month or week should feel free to assist as needs arise. As they sit in the assembly and sense the needs of a worshiping congregation, they provide a ready resource for the worshiper who needs to find her place in the hymnal, the parent who is looking for the restroom for his toddler, or the elderly saint who needs a strong arm to make her way up the steps to the communion table. Such assistance is offered in the name of *equipping the saints for the work of ministry, for building up the body of Christ.*

"

Rejoice with those who
rejoice, weep with those who
weep. Live in harmony with
one another.

Romans 12:15-16a

There's more
Sending the community to serve

With the regulars and the visitors greeted and seated, the offering received, the faithful guided to the table, one might assume that the duty of the greeter or the usher is completed for another week. But scripture does what scripture will always do: challenge us to see a bigger picture. Worship is over, but now our service begins in the world. A different script than that of the surrounding culture guides the ministry of ushers and greeters. There is still holy and important work to be done: ushers and greeters continue in this postservice script: *rejoice with those who rejoice, weep with those who weep. Live in harmony with one another.*

Once I visited a church where the participants told me, "At our place we de-greet." What they meant to convey was that they did as much community building on the way out of the service as they did on the way into it. I doubt that *de-greeting* will ever catch on as a moniker for what can happen in the attentive and caring congregation at the worship's end. But the idea of it does make clear that greeters and ushers still have work to do even after the assisting minister announces the dismissal and the congregation responds with its hearty, "Thanks be to God!"

There are the mundane chores of course: managing the recycling of paper resources, tidying the seats for the next service later that day or next Sunday. Ushers might direct people to coffee hour or other activities. They could be called on to hand out at-home devotional or parish announcements. They might even empty restroom trash cans for a subsequent service and make certain that the 11:00 service folks have fresh paper towels and toilet paper.

But some of the work, though subtle, continues that important ministry of brokerage discussed in chapter 2. This is an excellent time for people to be connected to one another in the community of Christ. How can the postworship time at your place of worship be a time of welcome and invitation? Who needs to be connected to whom? How can those trained in and volunteered for the ministries of greeting and welcome see these precious minutes as a time to continue their work of making God's people welcome, more deeply inviting them into the ministry of the gospel?

Visitors, especially first-time visitors, are often much more open to conversation and engagement now than they were before the service began. Having been made one in Christ through the word and the meal, our softened hearts are great ground to cultivate with the tenderness and love of which the gospel speaks. "Will you join us again?" "We loved having you with us." "By your presence we have come closer to Christ." "How can we help you?" Any of these sentences can serve as an opening to a deeper relationship and a deeper conversation about why we do the things we do together in Jesus' name. More importantly, they are invitations not only to reach out to others, but to allow others to form us in our ever-growing faith.

Having a knowledgeable and welcoming volunteer serve as a resource at a designated table or desk each week in the gathering space after service—perhaps before as well—is helpful to regular attendees and visitors alike.

From this post, such a volunteer, or perhaps even a paid employee such as a parish secretary or office manager, can offer materials useful to both new and old participants alike. He or she can manage sign-ups for activities, hand out parish resources, and gather information about pastoral care needs. This station and its resource person can free up the pastors to be able to greet as many people as possible, to do their own share of brokering now that the time of worship is completed. They will also have the freedom to be drawn into deeper conversation and immediate pastoral needs, which arms full of resources and responsibilities might otherwise prohibit.

The drama of worship does not end at the sending or the postlude. Now comes a transition time into the next act of ministry—this time moving from word to world. With scripture resounding in the ears of all and this postservice script for ministers of hospitality to follow with their final act of worship and praise, the community can be further equipped to take into a waiting world the good news of Jesus.

"
The Pharisees and their
scribes were complaining
to [Jesus'] disciples, saying,
"Why do you eat and drink
with tax collectors and
sinners?"

Luke 5:30

Coffee hour
This is (also) the feast of victory for our God

We ended the previous chapter with a call for the people of God to transition into their next act of ministry—moving the word into the world. But in most places where Lutherans gather there is an additional fueling stop—coffee hour.

The liturgy seems to suggest that we go directly from the Lord's table to the world with the good news of the gospel. The sending rite is brief. The assisting minister's direction is clear: "Go in peace. Serve the Lord." We robustly respond: "Thanks be to God." But rather than hitting the streets with the eucharist fresh on our breath and in our bellies, we take an instant sabbatical; we take a coffee break before we ever actually clock in for gospel work.

All that said, there is certainly great precedent in the scriptures for God's people eating and drinking together. Even Jesus enjoyed the opportunity. If we can see coffee hour as a time when our fellowship and conversation further equip and embolden our ministry in the world, then bring it on!

In the range of congregational experiences, coffee hour runs the gamut from a quick stand-up cup of coffee or glass of juice in the gathering area to a more formal, beautifully laid out spread of beverages and snacks, to a full blown congregational lunch. Whatever the case, whether simple or elaborate, there are a few things to keep in mind as hospitality teams and ministers plan for that "final act of worship."

Is the hospitality welcoming to all?

Is the way that people gather around good gifts to be shared and enjoyed something to which all who have worshiped feel welcomed and invited? Would visitors know how to find it? Are visitors graciously and genuinely encouraged to attend, or might coffee hour seem to them more like "family" time? This again might be a topic for a group of friends outside the congregation's direct faith community to observe and offer feedback on. A pastor could also ask visitors or relative newcomers from time to time of their impressions of welcome to the congregation's gathering for snacks and conversation.

Is the hospitality consistent with the congregation's values?

A liturgical celebration and sermon might call a congregation to care for the earth. To immediately follow with a coffee hour that is not thoughtfully planned would be inconsistent. Are fair trade coffee and other items served? Is the table spread with serving pieces that are detrimental to the environment (for example, Styrofoam cups, or noncompostable serving plates and utensils)? Are the foods offered healthy and nutritious, or are they treats filled with sugar, fat, and cholesterol? Certainly there are times for celebrations with our favorite foods, but a steady diet of offerings that model poor care of the body is inconsistent with the idea that our bodies are the temple of the Holy Spirit.

Is the hospitality multicultural and multigenerational?

How closely do the foods and beverages offered at coffee hour reflect those in attendance at worship? Are there offerings that are friendly toward and healthy for children? Alongside cookies and coffeecake, are there also options of vegetables and fruits, reflecting a sensitivity to people both young and old for whom *only* sugary treats may pose a mild or serious health problem? Do the foods and beverages reflect the cultural heritages and food preferences of those who attend or of those who might visit? Not everyone who attends a Lutheran congregation these days will recognize lefse or Pfeffernusse. More to the point, not everyone will feel a part of the whole if, week after week, these foods and their close cousins are the unvarying fare.

In keeping with the tradition of Jesus, who is well known to have eaten with tax collectors and sinners, as ministers of hospitality we might want to ask ourselves what sort of job we are doing of intermingling with those least like us. Coffee hour can become a coffee clique that certainly does little to strengthen our ministry in the world. With careful planning, conversation, and practice, barriers between generations, ethnic groups, socioeconomic groupings, longtime members, and newcomers can be effectively overcome. The well-trained ministers of hospitality realize that their role as "greeters" is not something that ends with the beginning of the worship service. Their role as "brokers" can and should be encouraged throughout this important time of coffee and conversation.

Providing kid-friendly snacks, activities, and supervision is also an important role of the hospitality team. In many congregations there is a sense of tolerant agitation that our youngest members wander off to remote places in the building or run around unsupervised. This is an adult challenge to face and solve, not one that the children themselves are able to navigate. Thoughtful planning of kid-friendly foods and furnishings help the youngest to feel welcome and supported. There might even be a wonderful opportunity during this time for cross-generational pairings: kids with youth group members or kids with surrogate grandparents. Can you imagine eighty-six-year-old Hannah next to four-year-old Jessica, sipping coffee and juice and sharing a snack but also coloring a page together that has an illustration from today's gospel reading? It may take some organization and planning to get off the ground, but such intention can lead to a rich and wonderful mix of God's people in fellowship *together*.

More than coffee

For the newcomer—especially the newcomer to faith—this time of fellowship and interaction is a time of socialization. The days are long gone when everyone *knows* what happens at all the gatherings of the church. Newly baptized adults, recent affirmers, or newly welcomed visitors among our congregational communities will benefit greatly from warm and welcoming invitations to join in the conversation, and from the leadership of their sponsors or others who have had primary responsibilities for assimilating them into the life of a disciple of Jesus.

Beyond our integration into the family of faith *inside* the church at coffee hour, wise parish leaders will plan social and refreshment time with an eye toward integration of those *outside* the walls of the building. When possible, and where feasible, coffee hour might be held outside— on the sidewalk of an urban congregation, the lawn of a suburban parish, the parking lot of a rural church. Not only could we let the neighbors see us, but we could invite them to join us. In certain settings, the opportunity to feed the hungry may be as close to our own eucharistic celebration as the coffee hour feast. It's an amazing opportunity to help the neighborhood know that we *live* the faith we profess.

Just as Jesus ate and drank with those least expected, so we too might use this time of hospitality and fellowship to reach those who could be most surprised by our embrace. What could be a more wonderful reflection for individuals or families leaving the church than to have their imaginations filled with the mental picture of new friends that were made, new neighbors who were welcomed, or new mouths that were fed? With such an open and welcoming plan in place for the weekly coffee hour's celebration, the whole of God's people again truly sing together, "This *is* the feast of victory for our God!"

I was a stranger and
you welcomed me.

Matthew 25:35

A final word
The importance
of welcome

In the city of Seattle where I live, Canlis is one of our finest restaurants. It is a family-run business. The family is unapologetically Christian, and they continue the pattern of being closed on Sundays, although it could obviously be a windfall day for them in a city as secular as ours.

The restaurant has an occasional online newsletter, and one of their recent publications caught my eye because of its theme of welcome.

As I read it, I thought about how clearly God was at work in this small, neighborhood family business, and how much their understanding of welcome and hospitality could help us in the church to deepen our sense of a truly open door.

Quoting owner Alice Canlis, the Service Director, the writer says:

> "We were all standing by the door in the foyer when she said, "Tonight they [the guests] will walk through our doors as strangers and leave as our guests. It's your welcome, your embrace that will transform them. This is hospitality: the invitation from unknown to known."[4]

This small volume has been offered in the hope that we as the people of God can take the time, muster the intentional practices, and foster the skills that will help us to move all who worship into a deeper relationship with one another and with God. In the words of the matriarch of the Canlis family, to move all who come through our doors from *unknown to known*.

It's not as easy as it sounds, but it is well worth the effort. In fact, it is a joyful task to which we are called as the people of God. Without the effort, we are not welcoming, but simply tolerating, as our local restaurateurs so aptly explain.

4 Canlis newsletter, summer 2014, http://canlis.com/canlisland/wp-content/uploads/2014/08/Canlis-Newsletter_Summer-2014_Paginated.pdf.

" In staff orientation we try to describe the difference between embracing a stranger and merely tolerating their existence. Somehow "tolerance" has become a social standard—a very low standard indeed. . . . But the trend towards tolerance is a well-intentioned movement with the wrong mascot. To tolerate means to endure, or allow, or put up with. Tolerance is for the detached, the isolationist, the man [*sic*] whose mind is permanently made up. Should we aspire to the ideal of tolerating one another we may find ourselves having left the world at arm's length, waiting for them to come around to our own point of view. Hospitality, by contrast, implies inviting the difference in and making space for it. Hospitality is not a call to endure, but to embrace.

In our business this is not as easy as it sounds.[5]

5 Ibid.

In our "business" it's not as easy as it sounds, either. But it is worth it. And the rewards of our efforts to welcome will deeply enrich our congregational ministry and our relationships with one another and with God. Jesus said, "I was a stranger and you welcomed me" (Matt. 25:35).

Appendix
The "Count Me In" form

A form such as this, or one more clearly tailored to your own local ministry needs, can be an important tool in welcome and hospitality. It can eliminate the need for many of the familiar but inadvertently unwelcoming gestures of many of our current ministry practices, such as the expectation to sign a guest book, the need to be counted in attendance at worship, or a communion card.

The Count Me In (CMI) form can also serve as a way of making an offering when the plate is passed. For those who otherwise choose *Simply Giving*, an annual gift, on-line giving via credit card or PayPal, the CMI becomes a way of truly offering themselves—with each worshiper's intentions of upcoming volunteer service in the parish included on the form. In this way the offering really isn't just about money, but about *time*, *talent*, and treasure.

Consider including a QR code on the form to allow those fully immersed in the use of technology to complete the form on a tablet or smartphone. Scanning the QR code takes the user to an online form where exactly the same information is shared, but in a keyed-in format.

What follows is a sample of a Count Me In form that could begin the conversation and imagination at your place of ministry. Don't be limited by this sample. Assess your own needs and design a format that serves your ministry in a unique and helpful way.

WELCOME TO WORSHIP
Fourth Sunday after Epiphany
January 29, 2017

Your presence at worship is important to God and to us! Whether you are a first-time visitor, frequent participant, neighbor, member, or friend, please take a moment as you prepare for worship to share some information. Place it in the offering plate at the time the offering is received, or if you prefer, use the QR code to share the information through your device.

Name: _____

Email: _____

Names of others with you:

_____

__ member __ first-time visitor __ repeat visitor __ participant/friend
__ I/we will receive communion today.

If you're new to us, or your contact information has changed and you'd like to share it:

Address: _____

Phone/s: _____

__ I'd like to know more about the congregation and its ministry.
__ Please add me to your mailing list.
__ I'd like a pastor to contact me.

COUNT ME IN

__ I'd like to become a Habitat for Humanity volunteer.

__ I'd like more information about Young Men's Bible Study.

__ I can assist with visits to the homebound on Saturday, March 18, 2017.

__ I'd like to purchase an Easter lily for the Easter Sunday worship environment
    __ in honor of_____.
    __ in memory of_____.
    (place a check in the offering, or use PayPal or a credit card on the church's website: www.yourlutheranchurch.org).

__ Please order me a copy of Bonhoeffer's *Life Together* for the April adult forum.

__ I have the following prayer request:

        __ please check here if it's okay to publish this prayer request in the bulletin.

For further reading

Duckworth, Jessicah Krey. *Wide Welcome: How the Unsettling Presence of Newcomers Can Save the Church.* Minneapolis: Fortress Press, 2013.

Huffman, Walter, C., and S. Anita Stauffer. *Where We Worship.* Philadelphia: Board of Publication, Lutheran Church in America, 1987.

Lathrop, Gordon. *Central Things: Worship in Word and Sacrament.* Minneapolis: Augsburg Fortress, 2005.

———. *The Pastor: A Spirituality.* Minneapolis: Fortress Press, 2006.

Nouwen, Henri J. M. *Reaching Out.* Garden City: Doubleday, 1975.